SPIRITUAL NIGHTLIGHTS

SPIRITUAL

Nightlights

MEDITATIONS FOR THE
Middle of the Night

LINDA K. DEVRIES

Harold Shaw Publishers
Wheaton, Illinois

ISBN 0-87788-743-8

Edited by Mary Horner Collins

Cover and inside design by David LaPlaca

Library of Congress Cataloging in Publication Data

DeVries, Linda K.
    Spiritual nightlights : meditations for the middle of the night / Linda K. DeVries.
      p. cm.
    ISBN 0-87788-743-8
    1. Insomniacs—Prayer-books and devotions—English. 2. Bible—Meditations. I. Title.
    BV4910.4.D48 1997
    242'.4—dc21   96-39578
                                                           CIP

02 01 00 99 98 97
10 9 8 7 6 5 3 2 1

For my mother, Doris Blackmun,
and my mother-in-law, Marian DeVries.

May their dreams of a good night's sleep come true.

Contents

Acknowledgments

My deepest thanks go out to some special people who made the writing and publication of this book possible:

To my husband, Dick, and my daughters, Taryn and Jill: You encouraged and supported me through this project from beginning to end, and you continually fill my life with love and joy.

To my invaluable critique group—Margaret Houk, Beth Ziarnik, and Pat Kohls: I am enthusiastically grateful for your skillful editing and moral support.

To many dear friends—you know who you are: I have treasured your fellowship and faithful prayers.

To all of you who have shared your stories of sleeplessness with me: Thank you!

And to my editors at Harold Shaw Publishers: Your excitement about this project has meant so much to me. I have appreciated your expertise and desire for excellence. Now Mary can get some sleep!

Most importantly, I acknowledge the Lord Jesus Christ, who planted the idea for these devotions in my mind and heart, then caused it to grow. May this work bear fruit for his kingdom and bring him glory.

Introduction

When you think about falling asleep, do you await it eagerly as a time of rest and renewal for the next day? Or do you dread bedtime, afraid you won't sleep?

Insomnia—the prolonged inability to obtain adequate sleep—can strike anyone at any time. If insomnia is part of your life, as it has been for me, it may comfort you to know that you are not alone. A recent Gallup survey found that nearly half of all adult Americans have at least occasional difficulty getting to sleep or staying asleep. This figure is up 13 percent from only a few years ago.

For a fortunate few, wakefulness is no big deal. These individuals clean cupboards, write letters, or catch up on their reading. I am not productive in the middle of the night, nor are most of the people I have talked to on the subject. We see sleeplessness as the nighttime monster of our childhood fears.

My insomnia, this uninvited and unwanted companion, came and went unpredictably for years. I prayed, "Lord, please get me through the night!" more times than I could count. Eventually, completely exasperated, I began to look through my Bible for every mention of "sleep" and "night." I found that God had a lot to say on those subjects. "The unfolding of your words gives light," says Psalm 119:130. The verses I studied shone as God's caring "nightlights" to me. I recorded them, pondered them, wrote about them. Thus, a book came into being.

I've come to terms with my now-occasional insomnia. When those nights stretch on forever, I no longer panic. Tomorrow will come eventually, so I can choose to wait it out or take action. I now have a reserve of information to draw on, and so do you. I've arranged these meditations topically for easier access. Rather than reading straight through the book, you may find it best to dip into portions that strike a chord with you right now. For those of you who suffer with chronic insomnia and wonder if you should pursue medical assistance, see "When and Where to Seek Professional Help" on page 141 for helpful information.

Achieving victory over occasional or chronic insomnia is not accomplished with an adrenaline-rush of excitement. It's more often done by gradually giving in to rest. We learn to relax, to make adjustments, to try new things. We invite the Lord into our wakefulness and rest in his arms. We listen to chirping crickets, distant train whistles, the swish of wind in the trees—sounds we miss in the noise of the day.

We begin to welcome the silence, night's gift to us. We embrace this silence and become comfortable with it. We allow the God who created us and who knows us best to speak to us and carry us through the hard times. We find the freedom of surrendering to our sleeplessness.

Now, as my daughter Jill used to say, "Sleep dreams!"

True Rest

Read Matthew 11:28-30.

> "Come to me, all you who are weary and burdened, and I will give you rest" (v. 28).

"Anxiety can be your best friend if it draws you into Christ's arms and the assurance of God's love for you," I heard a pastor say. Anxiety, our best friend? How ridiculous this sounds to a society plagued by excessive, persistent worries we can't seem to control. Over ten million Americans suffer from the effects of anxiety, with symptoms such as sleep disturbances, irritability, and lack of concentration. We can't seem to rise above our distress.

Therapists advise us to reduce this anxiety by talking with friends, improving our communication, staying positive with a sense of humor, and practicing good nutrition, exercise, and relaxation. For severe problems, they often prescribe medications to correct an imbalance of the chemicals in our brains.

While competent professional help is sometimes necessary, the first step for all of us in reducing stress is to respond to a special invitation: "Come to me," Jesus says simply. He welcomes all who are weary, overwhelmed, and burdened by anxieties to find true rest by walking alongside him. "Walk with me and work with me—watch how I do it. Learn the unforced rhythms of grace. . . . Keep company with me and you'll learn to live freely and lightly" (Matthew 11:28-30, *The Message*). What a promise!

Prayer

Lord, I come to you tonight to find rest. Teach me how to shed my anxieties and walk in step with you. Amen.

Keeping Perspective

Read Psalm 127:1-2.

"For he grants sleep to those he loves" (v. 2).

I had known Shelley only a short time, but we had something in common—sleeplessness. "When I can't sleep," Shelley told me, "I feel as if God doesn't love me. The Bible says God gives sleep *to those he loves*." Many of us have shared Shelley's fear. Our middle-of-the-night struggles with sleeplessness can easily distort our perspective on life and hardships. Is insomnia a sign of God's displeasure? Is God punishing us?

To better understand what this verse means, we need to explore the context of the entire psalm. This was a "psalm of ascent" which the Israelites sang as they made their annual pilgrimage "up" to Jerusalem. It called them away from their frantic anxiety over food and shelter and security from their enemies. As they walked along, the song slowly directed their focus back to God's sovereignty and care, leading to real rest.

It can do the same for you. When you can't sleep, check for underlying signs of anxiety that come from planning and worrying about life's necessities. Trust again in the Lord's love. As you take steps to trust in him as the sole source of your security and blessing, you will be able to see the futility of these thoughts that preoccupy your mind and keep you from sleeping.

Prayer

Forgive me, Lord, for my frantic efforts to provide for my own needs. Teach me to trust you and to rest in your loving care. Amen.

Forgetting to Worry

Read Matthew 6:25-34.

> "Therefore do not worry about tomorrow, for tomorrow will
> worry about itself. Each day has enough trouble of its own"
> (v. 34).

"Don't worry; be happy," a popular song told us. It made it sound so easy. But I struggle with worries that often consume me and make sleep impossible. I'm afraid to stop thinking about my concerns. What if I forget something important or take action without enough preliminary thought? So I lie awake and stew. Unfortunately, the same matters are still waiting for me in the morning, when I'm even less able to cope with them due to insufficient sleep.

I've tried different ways to "drain my brain" as I go to bed, just as I discard the day's dirt from my body with a daily shower. One method I've found effective is to write down each worry as it comes to mind, then set the list aside to deal with the next day. Sometimes I pray on paper, turning over my list of concerns to the Lord's care while I sleep. I don't have to worry about forgetting them because I have recorded them. Often a fresh solution comes to me in the morning—evidence that God is at work.

Fussing over everyday matters is unproductive. Jesus says, "Steep your life in God-reality, God-initiative, God-provisions. Don't worry about missing out. You'll find all your everyday human concerns will be met. Give your entire attention to what God is doing right now, and don't get worked up about what may or may not happen tomorrow. God will help you deal with whatever hard things come up when the time comes" (Matthew 6:33-34, *The Message*).

Prayer

Lord, help me let go of my concerns long enough to rest. May my faith in your care consume my worries, not the other way around. Amen.

From Fretting to Faith

Read Psalm 37:1-9.

"Do not fret. . . . Trust in the Lord and do good" (vv. 1, 3).

"Why do they get to do it and I don't? It's not fair!" my children complained. I uttered these words often myself as a child. My father would respond in a matter-of-fact tone, "Life *isn't* fair." As adults, we may be too sophisticated to express our thoughts in a childish whine, but we still yearn for our world to operate according to fairer standards—for good to be rewarded and evil to be punished. Our helplessness and frustration build as we think about the inequities of life, and this pushes sleep even further away.

In this psalm, King David struggles with the same dilemma. He observes that much of people's dissatisfaction comes from envying the prosperity of evildoers. In response, he repeats three times, "Do not fret." To *fret* means "to eat away; to become worried or irritable." Anger eats away our peace; envy gnaws at us. Left unattended, these feelings will seep into our emotional well-being and leave a residue of bitterness.

How do we rid ourselves of fretfulness, so we can rest? The psalm reminds us that people who don't follow God will soon vanish, while those who love and obey him will eventually receive the desires of their hearts. So don't worry about life's unfairnesses. Instead, direct your mind to other good things. Trust in the Lord. Do good. Get on with life, enjoying the place where you find yourself. Find delight in the Lord. Commit your way to him. Be still and wait patiently for him.

If envious thoughts are keeping you awake, try David's suggestions for banishing your fretfulness. You may not fall asleep immediately, but it will instill greater peace in your mind and heart.

Prayer

Lord, forgive me for envying the progress of others. Help me instead to trust in your eternal perspective. Amen.

Search and Destroy

Read Psalm 139:7-12, 23-24.

> "Search me, O God, and know my heart; test me and know my anxious thoughts" (v. 23).

Searchlights can be frightening. I always hold my breath during the scene of the film *The Sound of Music,* in which the von Trapp family hides in a convent from the Nazis. Family members crouch behind stone monuments while a searchlight moves across the stones. If a lock of hair or scrap of clothing protrudes, the von Trapps will be discovered and taken away to an unknown fate.

Searchlights illuminate everything in their path, uncovering and showing up what doesn't belong there. In view of this, Psalm 139 contains a courageous request. The psalmist asks God to shine his searchlight of truth into his heart. He asks God to illuminate the darkness there and destroy whatever shouldn't be there. He invites the all-knowing God to investigate every anxiety, because he knows that such thoughts have no place in a life of faith. As the Lord dissolves his worries, the psalmist can continue on his faith journey. He knows he won't be destroyed in the process; he will be purified and at peace.

Are you restless with anxious thoughts that are keeping you awake tonight? Ask yourself: *Am I willing to allow my heart and mind to be examined by God?* We may not like what we see when we open our lives to God's searchlight. It's hard to give up our anxieties. But remember, God is not out to search and destroy; rather, he refines us and lights up the path before us, dispelling the shadows of worry and doubt.

Prayer

Heavenly Father, search me and know my heart. Help me to bring my dark and anxious thoughts into your light and your loving care. Amen.

Money Matters

Read Ecclesiastes 2:22-26; 5:12.

> "The sleep of a laborer is sweet, whether he eats little or much, but the abundance of a rich man permits him no sleep" (5:12).

"Money is one subject that always keeps me awake," John said. "When I start mentally going over my family's financial future, I can't get to sleep."

"Thinking about money keeps me awake too," his wife, Sheila, admitted. "I'm always worried we won't have enough."

The writer of Ecclesiastes understood how preoccupied human beings can become about financial security. Centuries ago he wrote about such a person: "Even at night his mind does not rest." The greater our wealth, he observed, the greater our anxiety. And what we get from anxiously striving after riches are pain, grief, and sleepless nights.

Is it then a sin to be wealthy? No. The Bible speaks well of the prosperity of righteous people and encourages the blessing of sharing our wealth with others. But it also warns that preoccupation with wealth can separate us from God. "You cannot serve both God and Money," Jesus said (Luke 16:13), for "where your treasure is, there your heart will be also" (Matthew 6:21).

If you lie awake nights planning how to make more money or worrying about losing what you have, you probably won't sleep well. Consider where your real treasures are. God is the only true security, "for without him, who can eat or find enjoyment?"

Prayer

Lord, help me to remember at all times that you are the source of my wealth. I can trust you to care for me and my family. Amen.

Pray about Everything

Read Philippians 4:4-9.

> "Do not be anxious about anything, but in everything, by prayer and petition, with thanksgiving, present your requests to God" (v. 6).

" 'Twas the night before Christmas, when all through the house / Not a creature was stirring, not even a mouse. The children were nestled all snug in their beds / While visions of sugarplums danced in their heads." This scene from Clement Moore's classic poem sounds quite idyllic. But what about the parents of the household?

If they were anything like me, they hurried through all the last-minute holiday preparations. Then they fell into bed, only to be kept awake by their overtired bodies and anxious thoughts. Would little Janie like the gifts they had chosen for her? Would the weather cooperate, permitting their guests to arrive safely? Had they spent too much money? not enough? and on and on and on.

Anticipation may become a positive form of worry that keeps us awake. Preparing for such joyous occasions as a holiday celebration, the first day of school, a family vacation, or a wedding often contributes to sleepless nights. The apostle Paul encourages us to bring *all* of our concerns to God in prayer. Nothing is too insignificant.

This may prove difficult, but give it a try. Thank God in spite of your concerns, talk to him about them. And once you present your requests to God, don't grab them back. Relax and trust him to handle them for your good. That's where the peace is.

Prayer

Lord, the stress of happy times triggers anxious thoughts in me, just as the tough ones do. I give my concerns to you now with thanksgiving. Amen.

Remembering the Good

Read Psalm 77:1-12.

> "You kept my eyes from closing; I was too troubled to speak. I thought about the former days. . . . I remembered my songs in the night" (vv. 4-6).

My friend Laura learned that her husband's job was being moved, yet again. After many transfers, she had finally put down deep roots. Now she felt as if she were being pulled out of the ground too soon and against her will. She sank into depression, mourning her loss of place, asking God to change the situation and allow them to remain where they were. Like the psalmist, day and night she "stretched out untiring hands and [her] soul refused to be comforted" (v. 2).

In the face of similar troubled thoughts and unanswered questions, we read that the author of Psalm 77 found comfort in remembering the Lord's "miracles of long ago." Memories of God's love and faithfulness reassured him. He could appeal to the evidence of

God's record in the past. In the same way, as Laura reflected on God's faithfulness in her own life, she grew more confident that he had plans for her, wherever she found herself.

If you are feeling lost or troubled by changes and just can't sleep, take a moment to remember the "former days." Let God's faithfulness comfort you. Often the Lord asks us to call on the past to encourage us to move into the future with faith.

Prayer

Lord, when everything seems out of control, remind me of how you met my needs and desires in the past, and give me hope for the future. Change my nighttime tears to songs. Amen.

The Secret of Contentment

Read Philippians 4:12-13.

> "I have learned the secret of being content in any and every situation, whether well fed or hungry, whether living in plenty or in want" (v. 12).

Many of us spend a lot of time lamenting the "what ifs" and "if onlys" of our lives: What if I had married someone else? What if I had majored in drama instead of accounting? If only I had more money. If only I could get more sleep!

Such questions can cultivate a sense of discontent that saps the strength we need to cope with life's realities. The great preacher Charles H. Spurgeon noted this truth: "Anxiety does not empty tomorrow of its sorrows, but only empties today of its strength."

Living in a chronic state of anxiety can become such a habit that we feel guilty if we're not worried about something. To some extent, worrying shows we care enough to be concerned about something or someone, while the absence of worry indicates indifference. But worry also shows a lack of trust.

To break this pattern, try replacing your "what ifs" with thankfulness. In Christ the apostle Paul found the strength and grace to cope with and accept whatever happened to him. You can too. Remind yourself what is most important to you; allow lesser concerns to fade. Instead of wishing things were different, take action when and where you can. Counting your blessings when you feel shortchanged is a step toward contentment and rest.

Prayer

Lord, teach me the secret of contentment by trusting you with the circumstances of my life. Thank you that I can do all things through you. Amen.

Casting Off Cares

Read 1 Peter 5:6-11.

> "Casting the whole of your care—all your anxieties, all
> your worries, all your concerns, once and for all—on
> [God]; for He cares for you affectionately, and cares about
> you watchfully" (v. 7, *The Amplified Bible*).

My grandmother loved to fish. A small woman with fluffy white hair,
she would don her wide-brimmed straw hat, grab a casting rod, and
head out in a rowboat. Maybe she was drawn by the challenge of catch-
ing "the big one." Perhaps she enjoyed the quiet of the lake,
uninterrupted by the activities of daily life, and the soothing, repetitive
casting of the line into the water.

The verses above remind me of my grandmother. *Casting* is what
she did, whether she was fishing or bringing her worries to Jesus and let-
ting him take care of them. God wants us to literally throw our cares
into the water of his great love. The word *care* is used two ways in

1 Peter 5:7. The first time it refers to all *our* fearful concerns that hold us in their grip. The second use shows *God's* loving concern for his people. What a difference! My care is debilitating, while his care is life-giving.

We can't eliminate the problems in life, but we can refuse to be weighed down by them. Start by casting just one or two worries onto God right now. With his help, you will emerge "strong, firm and steadfast" (v. 10). Just the encouragement we need in the middle of the night.

Prayer

Lord, help me release into your loving care all the worries that are keeping me awake tonight. Thank you for your strength and grace. Amen.

Name That Fear

Read 2 Chronicles 20:5-17.

> "Do not be afraid; do not be discouraged. Go out to face them tomorrow, and the Lord will be with you" (v. 17).

King Jehoshaphat, ruler of the Israelites, received news that a huge enemy army was approaching from across the sea. He reacted much as I would—he panicked!

Then he took action. He proclaimed a fast and brought the people together to seek help from the Lord. By this time, war was imminent. The Israelites gathered in the temple courtyard to pray. They praised God for his sovereign power; they thanked him for past victories and for his promises for their future. They brought their specific fear of defeat to God and simply stated: "We don't know what to do, but our eyes are on you" (v. 12).

The Lord told them to face their enemy unafraid, because the "battle is not yours, but God's." They only had to get into position and stand firm, and they would see God go into action.

Unnamed fears often form an army and march into my mind in the middle of the night. They threaten my ability to capture a good night's sleep. Only when I'm able to put specific fears into words can I recognize them for what they are and talk to God about them. He reminds me—as he did the Israelites—to take up my position mentally and spiritually, to stand firm in faith, then to watch him work on my behalf. Then I shall rest.

Prayer

Lord, when I am afraid, show me that I don't have to fight the battle alone. Sometimes you want me to wait in faith and watch you win over my concerns and fears. Amen.

God's Sheltering Wings

Read Psalm 91:1-8.

> "He who dwells in the shelter of the Most High will rest in the shadow of the Almighty. . . . You will not fear the terror of night" (vv. 1, 5).

We've all heard the nursery rhyme prayer, "From ghoulies and ghosties and long-leggety beasties, and things that go bump in the night, Good Lord, deliver us!" Though it was probably written for children, adults who encounter more grown-up "beasties" recognize the relevance of its words. Nights can often be filled with alarming possibilities that cause worry and fear. It helps to form a battle plan to confront these terrors.

The psalmist uses some beautiful and vivid images of God's care for us: "in the shadow of the Almighty" and "in the shelter of the Most High." He describes how God "will cover [us] with his feathers," as we find refuge "under his wings." God's faithfulness is like a "shield and rampart."

The ability to picture a safe place to run when we face dangerous situations helps relieve our panic and allows us to think clearly. We especially need this refuge from our fears in the darkness of night. Choose one of these images from Psalm 91, or try envisioning one of your own, to meditate on. Rest assured that God will shelter you.

Prayer

Heavenly Father, because I can't see you, I sometimes forget that you are always with me. Thank you for your protection. Amen.

Be Still

Read Mark 4:35-41.

> "[Jesus] got up, rebuked the wind and said to the waves, 'Quiet! Be still!' Then the wind died down and it was completely calm" (v. 40).

A summer storm—blinding, noisy—blew into the night. I got up, shut the windows, then lay in bed wide awake until dawn. But it wasn't the crashes of loud thunder or the rain pelting against the house that kept me from sleeping. The true causes of my wakefulness were the thundering fears and downpours of anxieties roaring deep within me.

On a night long ago, Jesus and his disciples crossed the Sea of Galilee. Jesus had fallen into an exhausted sleep in the stern of the boat when an unexpected squall arose. (Jesus certainly had no trouble with insomnia!) His disciples—even though experienced fishermen—panicked as they fought to keep the boat from capsizing. Finally, they woke Jesus, begging him for help. "Don't just lie there—do something! Help us!"

Jesus instantly calmed the wind and water with his words, "Quiet! Be still!" His disciples suddenly realized the extent of Jesus' power. This was the very Son of God in their presence!

Sometimes I feel as though Jesus is "sleeping" through the storms in my life, unable or unwilling to do anything about them. I want him to yell, "Settle down!" to whatever upsets me. But when I remember who he is—the very Son of God—I worship him in awe and submission. In your storms tonight, turn to the Lord. Hear him say, "Why are you so afraid? I am here." Your difficulties may not subside instantly, but you'll be able to let go of your fears and find peace.

Prayer

Lord Jesus, help me when I doubt your interest in my welfare and your ability to care for me. You are the Son of God, and I rest in you tonight. Amen.

Marching Orders

Read Joshua 1:6-9.

"Do not fear. . . . Be strong and very courageous" (v. 6).

Have you felt overwhelmed with fears lately? Joshua could relate well to you. When God commissioned him to take Moses' place as leader of the Israelites, Joshua was perhaps apprehensive, even fearful, as he thought about leading God's people into the Promised Land. He may have lain awake nights contemplating whether he was up to the job. But the Lord anticipated Joshua's fears, and he empowered Joshua with both the strength and the courage he needed for this awesome task.

God gave Joshua some specific marching orders to ensure his success: "Do not let this Book of the Law depart from your mouth; meditate on it day and night, so that you may be careful to do everything written in it" (v. 8). To faithfully obey the Book of the Law's commands, Joshua would need to study and think about them constantly. They were to permeate his mind and heart and deeply affect how he lived. Then his mind would not be on the overwhelming assignment, but on following his Lord. And most important, God promised to be with him through it all.

Like Joshua, you may be fearing a task that lies ahead. Meditate on a part of God's Word, and you will draw closer to the mind and heart of God. Remember that God is with you, and you will gain courage to face tomorrow with confidence.

Prayer

Father God, guide me as I reflect on your Word tonight. Give me courage and strength for the work you have given me to do. Amen.

Not Afraid of the Dark

Read Psalm 3.

> "I lie down and sleep; I wake again, because the Lord sustains me. I will not fear the tens of thousands drawn up against me on every side" (vv. 5-6).

Nighttime brings its own dangers in every community, rural or urban. Crime has risen drastically, so that elderly citizens no longer feel safe, even in homes they have lived in for many years. Children in many cities around the world have grown up in war zones and cannot play safely outside. Refugees flee for safety from attacks in the night.

Centuries ago, King David also had reason to be afraid in the night. His son Absalom had launched a conspiracy to take his throne, and David had to flee Jerusalem, fearing for his life. As darkness approached, David cried out to the Lord. His prayers alternated between emotional cries for help and expressions of confidence that God would answer his prayers. His faith allowed him to lie down and sleep, even though he was surrounded by enemies looking for opportunities to kill him. David rested in God's faithful care, assured that he would wake to see the morning.

Think about the "enemies" that surround you, causing you to be anxious or restless tonight. These enemies may range from fear of death or violence to the fear of not living up to your own standards. Try to identify one or two and begin to pray as David did—honestly crying out to the Lord. Cling to any bit of confidence, however small, you have in God's ability to protect you. He will give you the courage you need to rest in his care. Our God is surely big enough to defeat our enemies.

Prayer

Lord, you alone can keep me safe. Help me lie down in peace, trusting in you for safety. Amen.

A Hiding Place

Read Psalm 32:6-8.

> "You are my hiding place; you will protect me from trouble and surround me with songs of deliverance" (v. 7).

In her book *The Hiding Place*, Corrie ten Boom tells the amazing story of how her family provided sanctuary for Jewish people during the German occupation of the Netherlands in World War II. When Corrie and her family were discovered by the German secret police, they were sent to concentration camps, where Corrie's father and sister died.

After years of internment and waiting and watching God work miracles in her life and in others' lives around her, Corrie was finally released. She dedicated the rest of her life to writing and speaking about those experiences, testifying to how the Lord protected her in the midst of great suffering. He had been her true "hiding place."

Are you afraid or suffering greatly right now? Take heart from Corrie ten Boom's story and reach out to the Lord. Ask him for protection and guidance. Listen for his call, for his wisdom and peace beyond any you can muster on your own. No matter what the situation, he will be with you.

Prayer

Lord Jesus, you are my true hiding place, no matter what happens. Help me rest in this truth tonight. Amen.

He Knows When You're Awake

Read Psalm 121.

"He who watches over you will not slumber" (v. 3).

A few years ago, I slipped on a patch of ice and broke my ankle. After several days in the hospital, I returned home plagued by the fear of falling again. Any thought of leaving the security of my house felt overwhelming. I refused opportunities to go out, and I lay awake nights pondering the calamities that might occur should I venture outside.

Then a friend drew my attention to Psalm 121. At first the words seemed contradictory to my experience. "He will not let your foot slip," says the psalmist. Well, my foot *had* slipped, and look what had happened as a result.

Then I read the rest of the verse: "He who watches over you will . . . neither slumber nor sleep." The psalmist was reminding himself—and so reminded me as well—that the Lord is continually watching over his people. The same God who made heaven and earth also watches over *my* "coming and going."

Christians are not guaranteed lives free from difficulty, but we can be sure that God will not desert us when we struggle. He never sleeps; he knows when we are awake and struggling with sleeplessness. His purposes for our lives cannot be hindered. If you are struggling with fear tonight, take time to meditate on this psalm. Allow God's Word to give you the courage you need to face tomorrow's challenges.

Prayer

Thank you, Lord, for watching over me and protecting me both day and night. Help me remember that you are always with me, whether I am awake or asleep. Amen.

Sweet Dreams

Read Proverbs 3:13-15, 21-26.

> "When you lie down, you will not be afraid; when you lie down, your sleep will be sweet" (v. 24).

"Sweet dreams," someone says as you head off to bed. *I wish I could have sweet dreams,* you think. *How can I dream when I can't even get to sleep?* And some people—perhaps you are one of them—can't sleep because they are afraid of dreaming. My neighbor, a therapist, believes that dreams are always "sweet" because they nurture us in some way. Dreams may comfort, teach, or make us aware of something we have been avoiding and need to confront. Even our most terrifying nightmares can prove helpful if we look for the truths they reveal.

The author of Proverbs, King Solomon, offers help for sleeping without fear. He suggests that we learn wisdom and follow the Lord's leading. This wisdom from God—understanding for right living—comes by simply asking him for it. We can also seek it from other people, books, and, yes, even our own dreams. "For God does speak—now one way, now another—though man may not perceive it. In a dream, in a vision of the night, when deep sleep falls on men, as they slumber on their beds" (Job 33:14-15).

God may reveal a truth to us at night when our conscious mind is at rest and more receptive. We don't need deep dream analysis to discover some measure of truth. By recording and thinking about what you dream, you will learn to welcome the dream process rather than fear it. Turn your "ear to wisdom and [apply] your heart to understanding. . . . For the Lord gives wisdom . . . and he protects the way of his faithful ones" (Proverbs 2:2, 6, 8).

Prayer

Heavenly Father, protect me as I dream tonight. Help me to face sleep unafraid, knowing that I am in your care. Amen.

Restless with Regret

Read Daniel 6:16-23.

> "Then the king returned to his palace . . . and he could not sleep" (v. 18).

Are you regretting something tonight? Afraid it's too late or afraid that you've made the wrong decision? Even kings lose sleep over bad decisions and moral dilemmas. The Bible tells about the night King Darius of Babylon greatly regretted a decision. His trusted adviser Daniel had disobeyed his decree, and the king was forced to seal him up in a den full of lions. Restlessly, Darius waited for morning.

At the first light of dawn, King Darius raced to the lions' den. Tentatively, he called out to Daniel, and much to his surprise, Daniel answered! While the king tossed and turned all night, Daniel had spent the night in the midst of ferocious lions and emerged unharmed. How was this possible? God had intervened on Daniel's behalf and sent his angel to shut the lions' mouths. Daniel publicly recognized that the

48

Lord's power had rescued him. King Darius joined in praising God for Daniel's deliverance.

Your regrets, like those of King Darius, may be as fearful as the lions that surrounded Daniel. Talk them over with God and put the consequences of your decisions in his hands. God remains in control of circumstances even when we "blow it." He can bring good out of even our worst situations.

Prayer

Lord, shut the mouths of the "lions" of regret that surround me tonight so I may rest. Forgive my thoughtless decisions and reverse their consequences for the good. Amen.

Conquering Fear

Read Romans 8:15, 31-39.

> "I am convinced that neither death nor life, . . . nor anything else in all creation, will be able to separate us from the love of God" (vv. 38-39).

In the darkness of night, our fears can cause "separation anxiety." We feel isolated, cut off from our family, friends, and God. As we wrestle with our fears, we may even question God's love for us.

The apostle Paul recognized the key role fear plays in people's lives. He wrote to believers in Rome, "You did not receive a spirit that makes you a slave again to fear, but you received the Spirit of sonship" (v. 15). When people put their faith in Christ, they are trading in their bondage to fear for the presence of the Holy Spirit, who is able to empower them to conquer whatever terrifies them.

What are some of your fears tonight? Paul lists some of the things the Christians in Rome dealt with: trouble, persecution, famine, nakedness, enemy attacks, death, the hazards of living in a dangerous world, powers on earth or in the spiritual realm, facing the present or future, moving far from home, and "anything else in all creation." Sound familiar? This list is just as relevant for us as it was for the first-century Roman Christians.

But we can overwhelmingly conquer fear because God is for us. His great love can turn our negative thoughts to dreams of optimism, turned toward an eternal perspective. When we concentrate on God's almighty power, we realize that no force that troubles us can ultimately win, because "nothing, . . . absolutely *nothing* can get between us and God's love because of the way that Jesus our Master has embraced us" (vv. 38-39, *The Message*).

Prayer

Help me, Lord, to find victory over my fears tonight, as I grasp and hold onto the truth of your all-encompassing love for me. Amen.

Safe in the Ark

Read Genesis 7:13–8:1.

> "But God remembered Noah and all the wild animals and the livestock that were with him in the ark" (8:1).

Sleeping away from home often brings sleeplessness, even for the best sleeper. Motel pillows are never quite like our own. Mattresses may be softer or harder or lumpier than what we are accustomed to. Unfamiliar noises and smells can distract us, making sleep almost impossible.

In light of this, consider Noah's first and only "cruise." His time on the ark was not a vacation to some exotic location, but was instead a journey of obedience to God. Noah was six hundred years old when he boarded the ark! Was he physically exhausted by the work of building the ark and then loading it with all forms of wildlife? Was he apprehensive or frightened about an unknown future? Was he burdened with grief for people he knew who had been swept away by the flood-waters and the loss of the world as he had known it? In addition to these concerns, Noah and his family probably fought off seasickness during their year aboard their floating hotel atop the crest of the great flood. Imagine trying to sleep amid the mooing, neighing, chirping, and howling of all the creatures traveling with them.

Whether or not they slept well, we do know that Noah's strong faith in God sustained him. God had found Noah to be "a righteous man, blameless among the people of his time." This uncomfortable cruise was God's means of deliverance. Noah and his family emerged from the ark ready to serve God, on an earth washed fresh and clean.

Is your sleep disturbed by strange noises, crowded conditions, or the rocky seas of uncertainty? Perhaps God hasn't spoken to you as clearly as he spoke to Noah centuries ago, but you can be sure that he has your best interests at heart. God loves you and will care for you as he leads you according to his plan.

Prayer

Lord, just as you remembered Noah, I know you remember me too, right where I am. Help me to see your plan for me beyond the discomforts of this night. Amen.

A Stone Pillow

Read Genesis 28:10-22.

> "Taking one of the stones there, he put it under his head and lay down to sleep" (v. 11).

An itch here, a twitch there. The pillow feels as hard as a rock. Sometimes as I toss and turn, I think about the Old Testament patriarch Jacob, who spent a night with an actual stone for a pillow! People in ancient times often slept on the ground with hard objects as headrests, but it still seems rather uncomfortable to my modern-day mind and body.

However uncomfortable, the night Jacob spent en route from Beersheba to Haran turned out to be quite eventful. He had an unexpected encounter with God. While Jacob slept, he dreamed of a stairway that reached from earth to heaven. Angels climbed up and down on it.

The Lord God spoke to Jacob, echoing his promise to give Jacob's children the Promised Land and to bless all peoples on earth through them. Then came a promise Jacob could find rest in: "I am with you and will watch over you wherever you go, and I will bring you back to this land. I will not leave you until I have done what I have promised you" (v. 15).

Early the next morning Jacob responded to the Lord's promise by setting up the stone that had "cushioned" his head as a memorial to the Lord. He consecrated the stone with oil and affirmed his father's God as his own.

How might you consecrate the place where you sleep, the "stone" on which you lie, to God's glory? Whether you are at home or away, you can dedicate your place of rest to the Lord.

Prayer

Father God, as I lie here tonight, bless my bed as a place where I can rest in your promise to be with me, whether I am asleep or awake. Amen.

A Fish for a Bedroom

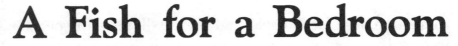

Read Jonah 1:17–2:10.

> "But the Lord provided a great fish to swallow Jonah, and Jonah was inside the fish three days and three nights" (1:17).

Tossing and turning are common to those of us who struggle with insomnia. We just can't seem to get comfortable, and this often makes us irritable. But remembering the story of Jonah gives new meaning to the phrase "tossing and turning." Running away from God, he had been thrown off his ship to calm a fierce storm. He had a near-death experience in the depths of the sea. Seaweed wrapped itself around his head as he descended.

Just when Jonah was about to die, God sent a great fish to swallow him. He remained in the belly of that fish for three days and three nights. In spite of this indescribable environment, Jonah saw how God mercifully had delivered him from a watery grave. As a result, he offered him praise and thanksgiving.

When you can't sleep due to discomfort or entanglements of one kind or another, cry out to the Lord. Try praising and thanking him in your wakeful hours, as Jonah did. Look for ways that God has rescued you. No matter how uncomfortable you are, refocus your thoughts on who God is and what new direction he may want to lead you.

Prayer

Sovereign Lord, even as I toss and turn, I acknowledge your love and provision for me. Help me to be obedient to your perfect will. Amen.

Hunger Pains

Read John 6:35-40; 7:37-39.

> "Then Jesus declared, 'I am the bread of life. He who comes to me will never go hungry, and he who believes in me will never be thirsty' " (6:35).

A hungry body demands to be fed, and its insistence keeps the most adept sleeper wide awake. If you've started a diet, run out of grocery money, or begun fasting for medical or spiritual reasons, your hungry stomach may be causing your wakefulness tonight. Or maybe your emotionally hungry heart is crying out for some kind of comfort food.

Jesus made a distinction between the kind of food that feeds the body and that which sustains the soul. Jesus knew what it was like to be physically famished. He had once fasted for forty days and nights in the desert. But he also knew that human beings don't live on bread alone, "but on every word that comes from the mouth of God" (Matthew 4:4). Frederick Buechner observes that our need to eat "reminds

us of other kinds of emptiness that not even the Blue Plate Special can touch."

Jesus promised that if we believe in him, our soul's hunger pains will be eased. So tonight you may need to go to the kitchen and eat something to quiet your rumbling stomach. But don't forget to also consider going to Jesus, the Bread of Life, who knows what you lack and can fill your deepest needs.

Prayer

Lord, fill me with your Spirit, with faith, and with whatever nourishment I need tonight. Amen.

How Long?

Read Job 7:3-5.

> "Nights of misery have been assigned to me. When I lie down I think, 'How long before I get up?' The night drags on, and I toss till dawn" (vv. 3-4).

Most of us are familiar with the suffering of Job, a blameless man who "feared God and shunned evil." Yet God allowed Satan to test him. Job lost his family, his livestock, his property, his health. He endured the accusations of three "friends," who considered his losses the direct result of sinfulness on his part. Despite his intense suffering, Job did not curse God.

Sometimes the intensity of our suffering can't be measured. Does your night drag on as Job's did? Has your bed become a place of misery? Like Job, any sufferer who believes in a loving, good, and sovereign God will struggle with the mystery of unjust suffering. Our earthly perspective prevents us from seeing the divine struggle behind our misery. We may never know why we experience our current distress.

The Bible tells of several people besides Job who confronted God: Jacob, David, and Jeremiah, to name a few. In his book *Space for God*, Don Postema writes of this human interaction with God as a sign of relationship and faith: "When I struggle, it feels like I am close to God, as close as when I argue with my family or friends." Certainly Job was one who struggled with God, begging for understanding, relief, and even death.

God did not abandon Job. He won't abandon us either. As he helped Job endure his suffering, so he will strengthen and uphold us in ours.

Prayer

Thank you, Lord, that you are not offended by my honest questions. Even when I can't understand why I am suffering, help me not to lose confidence in you. Amen.

God Hears

Read Psalm 6:1-10.

> "My soul is in anguish. . . . I am worn out with groaning;
> all night long I flood my bed with weeping" (vv. 3, 6).

I was visiting Anna in the hospital. With tear-filled eyes, she told me, "I'm eighty-three years old. I love the Lord, and now I would rather go home to heaven than suffer anymore." Her anguish and confession reminded me of the psalmist's prayer: "How long, O Lord, how long?"

I fed Anna a few ice chips, talked with her, and combed her hair. Then I took her hand to pray that she would receive comfort. No sooner had I begun to speak than the telephone rang. Her granddaughter was calling to check on her, a call that brought the first smile to Anna's face I had seen that day. When she hung up the phone, I took her wrinkled hand again and began to pray—this time that the doctor would come soon, which was Anna's fervent desire. I had just begun

when someone entered the room. I sighed, annoyed. Why were we being constantly interrupted?

That "someone" was the doctor. Later, as I stepped into the hall, I realized that God was answering my prayers even before I began to pray! How reassuring to know that we don't need to complete our prayers with a proper "Amen" for God to hear and answer.

Do you hesitate to pray for fear your words won't be eloquent enough? Are you having difficulty articulating your concern or request? God wants us to come to him in faith, humbly asking for what we need and want. He listens to our words but hears our hearts.

Prayer

Lord, my prayers are not always perfectly worded, but I know that you hear even my silent cries of distress. Thank you for working things out even as I begin to pray. Amen.

Who's in Control?

Read Psalm 30:1-12.

> "Weeping may remain for a night, but rejoicing comes in the morning" (v. 5).

A free weekend in midsummer lay ahead, and the weather looked promising. I began to plan some activities for our family to enjoy—a day at the beach, a picnic with friends. But Friday evening had barely begun when I came down with a stomach virus. I pleaded, "Lord, please take away this illness so we can get on with our plans." However, in the wee hours of the morning, I was still sick and still awake. In weakness and humility, I changed my request to "Lord, give me your strength to lean on, and help me to follow where you lead."

There is nothing quite like an illness—serious or not—to shake us out of our self-reliance. When we are healthy, we tend to rely on ourselves and our own strength. As life hums along, we slip into the practice of making plans without much thought to how they fit into

God's purposes for our lives. We feel in control. Then a twenty-four-hour virus hits—or something much worse—and our plans crumble. Quickly our lives feel out of control.

King David admitted to falling into this trap. In Psalm 30:6 he said, "When I felt secure, I said, 'I will never be shaken.' " But when his health left him, he lost confidence and cried out to the Lord for mercy and help.

Are you learning greater dependence on the Lord in your dark night of illness? Gather up your disappointments, your shattered plans, and your suffering, and offer them up in a prayer for God's mercy. As with David, over time your cry for mercy may become a psalm of praise to your Deliverer, who is in control: "You turned my wailing into dancing; you removed my sackcloth and clothed me with joy, that my heart may sing to you and not be silent. O Lord my God, I will give you thanks forever."

Prayer

O Lord, help me depend on you for direction and strength. I long for you to remove my suffering and clothe me with joy. Amen.

Good Medicine

Read Proverbs 17:22.

> "A cheerful heart is good medicine, but a crushed spirit dries up the bones" (v. 22).

"When I was hobbled by a disease of the connective tissue, . . . a few minutes of solid belly laughter would give me an hour or more of pain-free sleep," author Norman Cousins wrote in his book *Head First: The Biology of Hope*. Without dismissing the benefits of medical science, Cousins has long advocated the therapeutic value of laughter and other positive emotions in both physical and emotional healing. Medical research has substantiated his theory.

There are a vast number of medications available today that can alleviate some symptoms of illness but that don't really cure our ailments. During times when pain or sickness keep us awake and nothing will ease our discomfort, we often feel helpless and discouraged. How do we obtain a cheerful heart and laugh when we're feeling crushed?

In his book *Growing Strong in the Seasons of Life*, Chuck Swindoll suggests three simple assignments as a prescription to bring back our sense of humor and "yank us out of the doldrums": (1) Decide to start each day with pleasant words (even if you haven't slept). (2) Determine to smile more often. (3) Think of one honest comment of appreciation or encouragement to give each person you will see the next day.

If we practiced this prescription along with Cousins' "laugh therapy," I wonder how much better we would feel. Try it and see.

Prayer

Lord, I'm so tired of coping with this pain (or illness) with no relief in sight. Create in me a cheerful heart to replace my crushed spirit and ease my distress. Amen.

When God Says No

Read Isaiah 38:9-20.

> "I waited patiently till dawn, . . . day and night you made an end of me. . . . I looked to the heavens. . . . O Lord, come to my aid!" (vv. 13-14).

My neighbor Jeanne lies in a hospital bed awaiting a bone-marrow transplant. Members of her church join with her family and friends in praying for her healing. I believe God will answer our prayers, but maybe not in the way we desire. On this side of heaven the final outcome of Jeanne's story may not have a "happy ending." Yet as long as her struggle continues, we who care about her have hope, and we pray.

Many of us can tell exciting stories of miraculous healings. But we also know of times when God has not healed and apparently says no to our requests. What makes the difference? We may never know why one person is healed and another is not. King Hezekiah experienced both yes and no.

When King Hezekiah lay seriously ill, God sent the prophet Isaiah to tell the king to get his house in order and prepare to die. God's will was clear. Yet Hezekiah decided to make one last attempt at recovery. He cried out to the Lord, his fervent prayer mingling with his tears. God chose to add fifteen years to his life and even gave the king a supernatural sign to confirm his promise. Sometimes God does intervene in supernatural ways.

Other times God's answer is for us to endure our affliction. The apostle Paul prayed three times that his "thorn" of suffering would be removed, but the Lord said, "My grace is sufficient for you, for my power is made perfect in weakness" (2 Corinthians 12:9). God wanted to teach Paul to rely on God's grace.

You may be very ill as you read King Hezekiah's testimony tonight. Although you don't know how God will answer your prayers, ask him for healing and be confident that he will do what is best on your behalf.

Prayer

Thank you, Lord, for answering Hezekiah's prayer as a sign of hope and encouragement. Please hear my prayer tonight and bring renewed health or spiritual healing, whatever is your will for me. Amen.

Hope in Our Disability

Read Romans 5:1-5.

> "We also rejoice in our sufferings, because we know that suffering produces perseverance; perseverance, character; and character, hope" (vv. 3-4).

"Rejoice in our sufferings"? That was the last thing Joni Eareckson Tada wanted to do. A diving accident at age seventeen had left her paralyzed, a quadriplegic. It took years of struggle, but God's love did not disappoint her. Now, thirty years later, she directs a national ministry, Joni & Friends, helping individuals who are disabled. Out of her own suffering she brings hope and encouragement to others.

We all know people with challenging illnesses and disabilities. Perhaps you are one of them. How happy each person is usually depends on an ability to gain a wider perspective and to believe that God is in control. The verses above tell us that God can use suffering to bring good into our lives, qualities like perseverance, character, and hope.

These traits can help us live lives filled with joy, lives that can touch others in positive ways.

Are you lying awake, struggling with an illness or disability tonight? Be assured that, with time, God can use your particular circumstances, no matter how grim, to develop within you a stronger character, more perseverance, and greater hope. Ask him to pour out his love on you, and to help you in some way share his love with others.

Prayer

Father, I confess that I would rather not go through the pain and suffering it takes to develop character. Fill me with hope so I can persevere in living out your will for my life. Amen.

Together in Prayer

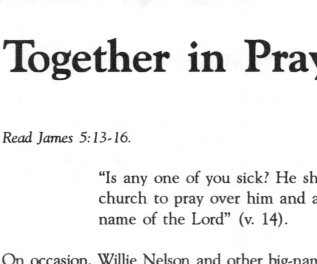

Read James 5:13-16.

> "Is any one of you sick? He should call the elders of the church to pray over him and anoint him with oil in the name of the Lord" (v. 14).

On occasion, Willie Nelson and other big-name entertainers bring their musical talents together under the banner "Farm Aid" to support financially troubled farmers. Their concerts raise more money for the cause when they perform together than when just one celebrity appears alone. Similarly, the Bible confirms the power of prayer when offered by a group of Christians together. Jesus told his disciples, "Where two or three come together in my name, there am I with them" (Matthew 18:20).

The verses above note the importance of community prayer in both physical and spiritual healing. James mentions several types of prayer: prayers for help in times of trouble, prayers of praise, intercessory prayers for healing, and prayers of confession. When we are sick, we are acutely aware of our need for support and relief. We need other people to provide strength when we are weak. But it takes humility and faith, as well as a desire to be healed, to ask others to pray with and for us.

When we pray together, we affirm more strongly God's power to heal, we support one another through the process of confessing our sins, and we help one another accept God's answer—whatever it may be. Praying together aids the process of restoration and healing.

You don't have to deal with your illness or insomnia alone. Whom can you ask from your church to support you in prayer? If you are not part of a Christian community per se, is there anyone else you can call who would be willing to come pray with you? There's power in togetherness.

Prayer

Lord, give me the courage to ask others to pray for me when I am weak. May I be faithful to pray with and for others as well. Amen.

Midnight Math

Read Psalm 25:15-21.

> "Turn to me and be gracious to me, for I am lonely and afflicted. The troubles of my heart have multiplied; free me from my anguish" (vv. 16-17).

Anyone who has difficulty sleeping can readily relate to this psalm written by David during the loneliness of night. Finding ourselves awake when everyone else in our time zone is asleep (so it seems) leaves us vulnerable. Troubles seem to multiply in our mind at an alarming rate, and our enemies—real or imagined—increase exponentially. Without another person awake to help us keep things in perspective, we can easily identify with David's feelings. His prayer can be a model for our own.

David begins by remembering that God is with him when no one else is. He affirms that God is able to rescue him from his distress. Then, boldly yet humbly, he calls on the Lord to observe his situation.

He asks for divine pardon and seeks refuge. Finally, he looks forward in God-centered hope.

Why not try writing out Psalm 25 as your own prayer tonight? Personalize it by inserting your name wherever the words *I*, *my*, and *me* appear. List your "enemies" (v. 19); confess your particular sins (v. 18). Somehow, when we have a pen in hand we feel less alone. We travel in company with people like David who have gone before us, people who have found hope as they struggled in the night.

Prayer

Lord, at night my troubles and enemies seem to multiply. I need you to watch over me. Take away my sins and my loneliness, for my hope is in you. Amen.

Never Alone

Read John 16:31-33.

"I am not alone, for my Father is with me" (v. 32).

Sarah looked tired. "When I can't sleep in the middle of the night," she told me, "and need someone to talk to, I can't just wake up my husband and start dumping all my concerns on him. And I don't think my friends would appreciate it if I called them on the phone at that hour."

I empathized with Sarah. When I can't sleep, sometimes a cloud of loneliness descends on me. My husband, sound asleep, is no company, nor are my sleeping children. When I was young, I could call my parents, and one of them would come to reassure me. Now I do most of the comforting.

At Jesus' darkest moment, when he faced the cross and death, his disciples deserted him and scattered to their own homes. Rather than feeling sorry for himself or getting angry, Jesus turned to his heavenly Father for company and comfort. We can learn from his example.

76

When I gaze out across my neighborhood on a sleepless night, I rarely see lights shining from other windows. I feel alone and vulnerable. During such times, I find companionship by reading the Bible or a favorite book. Sometimes I write prayers in a notebook, which gives me something tangible to hold onto as I direct my thoughts toward God. Try these approaches for yourself in your dark moments and discover if they help you feel less alone and closer to our caring God.

Prayer

Lord Jesus, help me to experience the close fellowship you had with your Father, so I can know with confidence that I am never alone. Amen.

The Lord, My Pillar

Read Exodus 13:21-22.

> "By day the Lord went ahead of them in a pillar of cloud to guide them on their way and by night in a pillar of fire to give them light" (v. 21).

After their hurried escape from Egypt, where they had lived as slaves, the Israelites found themselves wandering in a desert. They faced dangers of all kinds—they knew the Egyptian army would pursue them, and the Red Sea blocked the way before them. I can imagine them saying to each other fearfully, "What have we done? Here we are alone in the desert, and we don't even know exactly where we're going. Has God deserted us?"

But God was working out his sovereign plan for his people, and he would not abandon them. To assure them of his presence, he gave them two signs that would always be visible: a pillar of cloud by day and a pillar of fire by night. Whenever the people felt alone or afraid, they could look to that pillar of cloud or fire and know that God was there with them, guiding and watching over them.

A beautiful old hymn by Katherine Davis proclaims: "His banners are o'er us, his light goes before us, a pillar of fire shining forth in the night." You may feel especially alone or overwhelmed tonight, wandering in your own sort of desert. Take courage and remember how God showed his presence to his people at night in a pillar of fire. Ask God for your own sign of his steady and strong presence in your life.

Prayer

Father, when I feel alone, help me to recognize your presence with me. Be my pillar of fire during my sleepless nights. Amen.

Family Ties

Read Psalm 68:4-6.

"God sets the lonely in families" (v. 6).

Do you feel family-less tonight? Perhaps you are recently widowed or divorced. You may be an "empty-nester"—your children have left for college, jobs, or marriages. Or perhaps you've been unable to bear children. Maybe you moved to a community far from friends and family. You might be a Christian believer among people who don't share your faith in God.

Many people in the Bible found themselves in similar lonely circumstances. Moses was forced to flee to a strange land as a young man and lived an isolated shepherd's life there. Ruth and her mother-in-law, Naomi, were two widows who made a long, lonely journey back to Naomi's homeland after their husbands died. We read that, in time, God opened up new and different families for these migrants. God gave Moses a home that eventually included a wife, children, and a wise father-in-law (Exodus 2:11-22). Ruth found a new husband and gave birth to a son, and Naomi shared in the childrearing (Ruth 4:13-16).

God understands our feelings of loneliness. He calls himself a "father to the fatherless, a defender of widows," and he "loves the alien." He stays close to those whose loneliness brings pain.

Think about the alternative "families" God may have given you. Some people who live many miles from their biological family find that their church community becomes a family to them. Is there a small group in your church you could join? Is there a local organization of like-minded people you could investigate? Can you invite others into your home for a holiday celebration? God can and will provide new avenues of relationships where you are.

Prayer

Lord, I know that you are always with me. Help me to sense your presence tonight. Fill the emptiness in my heart. Amen.

Creative Loneliness

Read Isaiah 58:6-11.

> "Then your light will break forth like the dawn, and your healing will quickly appear; then your righteousness will go before you, and the glory of the Lord will be your rear guard" (v. 8).

Many books, poems, and hymns have been written by people who struggled with loneliness through sleepless nights and poured out their thoughts on paper. World-changing dreams and ideas have been born in the silent solitude of the night. Many a lonely heart, racked with sleeplessness, has reached beyond itself and developed deeper compassion for suffering people and greater peace within.

Dag Hammarskjöld, former secretary-general of the United Nations, encouraged people to use their times of loneliness to push themselves toward higher purposes in life. "Pray that your loneliness may spur you into finding something to live for, great enough to die for," he said.

God can lead us to use our loneliness for creative and loving purposes. The prophet Isaiah called on the Israelites to show their love for God by acting compassionately toward people who were oppressed, hungry, homeless, or naked. In return, God promised to bless them by illuminating their darkness, refreshing their parched spirits, and answering their prayers.

As you wrestle with your loneliness tonight, you might consider the possibilities of your own "high calling." What new ideas are hiding in the shadows of your mind, just waiting to be discovered? How might you help someone in need? By giving to others, you move naturally from isolation to connection.

Prayer

Heavenly Father, loneliness makes me feel so self-centered. Draw me away from this preoccupation with myself and show me how to reach out to those around me. Amen.

A Constant Companion

Read 2 Timothy 4:9-18.

> "Everyone deserted me. . . . But the Lord stood at my side and gave me strength" (vv. 16-17).

Have you ever watched a child eat alone in a school cafeteria? It tugs at our heartstrings to see his longing glances at groups of students who are laughing and sharing their lunches. Eating is a social activity. Meals provide opportunities for conversation and fellowship. Men and women who lose their spouses can often find mealtimes alone so difficult that they do not cook properly or sit down to eat. Similarly, people who dine alone in restaurants sometimes feel conspicuous and out of place.

How did the apostle Paul handle being alone after his friends deserted him? Countless times Paul was arrested and jailed. One particular time, he appeared in front of Caesar's court to defend his case alone. Then he was put in a cold prison with visits only from his friend Luke. Paul had plenty of reason to feel deserted and angry. Yet Paul did not get bitter. "May it not be held against them," he wrote. Somehow he was able to see beyond the absence of friends and family to feel Christ's presence, giving him strength to face his many challenges. He focused on proclaiming the gospel message, not on his loneliness.

If the loneliness of being awake at night becomes difficult for you, get acquainted with another insomniac. You could pray for one another during your wakeful times and encourage each other in the daytime, sharing books and advice that have helped you. Don't let despair or anger or bitterness stand in the way of asking friends, or God, to help you through a lonely time.

Prayer

Lord, thank you for being my constant companion both day and night. Reassure me of your continuous presence, and show me how to make the isolation of wakeful nighttime hours less lonely for myself and others. Amen.

When God Seems Far Away

Read Psalm 22:1-11.

> "My God, my God, why have you forsaken me? Why are you so far from saving me, so far from the words of my groaning?" (v. 1).

The need to know that we are not alone in our worst moments churns in every human heart. King David, the author of this psalm, was no different. He followed God and was known as a "man after God's own heart." Yet here he felt lost and abandoned, as if God had turned his back on him. David never dreamed that his words would be repeated centuries later. Jesus echoed this psalm at his death on the cross, crying in anguish, "My God, my God, why have you forsaken me?" Even the Son of God felt the agony of separation from God.

We think we believe in God. We *say* we believe in God. But sometimes living out that belief is hard. What do we do when God seems millions of miles away? when we can't "feel" his presence? when he responds with silence to our heartfelt prayers in the dark of night?

If you are feeling as if God has abandoned you, take comfort in knowing that Jesus understands your distress and cares about your pain. Read through Psalm 22. It will remind you that God does hear: "He has not hidden his face from [us] but has listened to [our] cry for help" (v. 24). He does not leave us alone in our darkest hours, but is present with us, as he was with those who trusted him in the past.

Prayer

Lord, you seem so far away when I am sad. Yet I ask you with confidence: Hear my prayer tonight and lift my heavy spirit. Amen.

Through the Tears

Read Psalm 42:1-11.

> "My tears have been my food day and night, while men say to me all day long, 'Where is your God?' . . . By day the Lord directs his love, at night his song is with me" (vv. 3, 8).

People who struggle with depression will find a kindred spirit in Psalm 42. Here the psalmist records his own emotional struggle in vivid language, directed toward both God and himself. His emotions swing back and forth between doubt and hope, despair and trust.

The psalmist looked back at the joy and thanksgiving he experienced in the past, when he led the procession to the temple. Yet now he feels alone, forgotten by the One who had received his praise. His fellow worshipers have been replaced with mockers, enemies who oppress him, taunt him, and question his faith. His tears spent, he is left with a deep thirst for God. He probably lost some sleep as his anguish swept over him like water over waterfalls.

Many of us identify with the psalmist's longing to feel God's presence and receive his encouragement. It's hard to maintain our hope and faith when God seems far away, when grief or despair overwhelms us. Sometimes we feel too weak to stand up under the onslaught of others' doubts and jeers.

In these times, the Bible reminds us who God is and what he has done for us. In prayer we can invite him into our sadness, confident that he hears our deepest sighs as well as our most joyful songs. And by speaking to ourselves in positive words, we echo the psalmist's expression of hope: "I will yet praise him, my Savior and my God."

Prayer

Heavenly Father, keep me from being overwhelmed by my unpredictable and ever-changing emotions. Please hear my cry tonight and restore my hope. Amen.

89

Grieving with Hope

Read 1 Thessalonians 4:13-18.

> "Brothers, we do not want you to be ignorant about those who fall asleep, or to grieve like the rest of men, who have no hope" (v. 13).

When we lose a loved one to death, time comes to an abrupt halt. Pain and grief surge over us. Even if we are confident that our loved one is with the Lord, the agony of missing him or her often keeps our eyes from closing, our thoughts from focusing, our bodies from resting.

Grief is a natural human response to death and loss. We all pass through the same stages of grief and experience the same tears. But there is one significant difference: those who believe in Christ grieve with hope. The apostle Paul wrote about this hope in hopeless times. He assures all Christians that when we die, we will be together with the Lord—and with our believing loved ones—forever! "Encourage each other with these words," Paul says.

Hope focuses on the future, on eternity. Hope brings us through painful periods of loss. We aren't ignorant of what is to come. God has let us in on a wonderful secret—Jesus is coming back again, there is a heaven, and believers will go there when we "fall asleep" for the last time on this earth. He made this hope possible through his Son, Jesus Christ.

Are you weary with grief tonight? Try to look beyond the present and catch a small glimpse of the shining light of eternity, when you will see Jesus and be reunited with those you love who have gone on before you.

Prayer

God, as I close my eyes, may I see the light of your presence. Help me rest in your promises of eternal life. Amen.

A Heavenly Comfort Zone

Read John 14:1-7.

> "In my Father's house are many rooms; if it were not so, I would have told you. I am going there to prepare a place for you" (v. 2).

My father-in-law was a carpenter. Over the years he built homes for many people, including his family. When he died, the family chose the above text from John 14 for his funeral service. He had gone on to his place in the heavenly Father's house, the one that Christ had built for him.

But when someone we love dies, their loss shatters our customary comfort zones. We no longer feel secure in our usual life routines of eating, sleeping, working, and playing. Nights seem especially interminable. Facing darkness knowing that our loved one is gone intensifies our pain.

Our sorrow, though painful, can be eased by the promise of heaven Jesus gives us in these verses. He urges us: "Do not let your hearts be troubled. Trust in God; trust also in me."

92

My family found rest in these words. Dad was with the Lord in heaven, and we would join him someday. The promise of an eternal place with God gave us a new "comfort zone" in which we could grieve and at the same time be assured of God's care.

As you read these verses tonight, be assured that Jesus himself walks with you through your grief and pain, and that he will lead you to your comfort zone, whatever the cause of your sadness.

Prayer

Lord Jesus, I seek comfort in your words tonight. Lift my sad heart, and help me to trust in you both for life here on earth and for life to come. Amen.

Thanks at Midnight

Read Psalm 119:57-64.

> "At midnight I rise to give you thanks for your righteous laws" (v. 62).

Sometimes I become a midnight prowler in my own home when I can't sleep. I find myself wandering down a familiar hall, tiptoeing through familiar rooms, gazing out at a familiar landscape transformed by the night. I look in at my sleeping children, and my heart overflows with love for them even as I envy their carefree slumber. Perhaps I open my Bible and turn to familiar and soothing passages, or read other materials. Then I crawl back into bed, and my husband barely stirs; his familiar breathing continues deep and steady.

It's frustrating to be awake. Yet I am thankful for my nocturnal wanderings through the familiar. I've lain awake night after lonely night in a hospital bed, sick and afraid. I've spent vacation nights in motel rooms with my family, suffering silently so as not to disturb their sleep.

I've been a guest in homes where I couldn't navigate the unfamiliar in the darkness, so I fitfully counted the minutes till dawn in a bed unaccustomed to my body.

So tonight I am thankful for the familiar—my home, my family, and God's Word. There is peace in realizing a sense of belonging that releases anxiety and yields contentment. I can rest in it. Take time to think about the ordinary things in which you find comfort, and thank God for them.

Prayer

Lord, thank you for the comfort of familiar surroundings and for the solace of your never-changing Word. Amen.

Sing and Cling

Read Psalm 63:1-8.

> "On my bed I remember you; I think of you through the watches of the night. . . . I sing in the shadow of your wings" (vv. 6-7).

One wakeful night I grew exhausted as my thoughts flitted from one concern or idea to another. And another. And another. The process reminded me of the ruby-throated hummingbirds that drink from our feeder each summer. They spend only a few seconds at each drinking hole, then they are off to sip nectar from a brightly colored flower, their tiny wings a blur. But while a hummingbird receives nourishment as it flits from here to there, my mind succeeded only in losing its focus as it lit on one worry after another. I found no rest.

Various people have told me that singing helps direct their thoughts and settle their hearts at frazzling times like these. As my friend Mary prepared for surgery, she memorized praise songs and

Scripture-set-to-music. This relaxed her and helped her cling to the Lord as the time for the operation approached and through the discomfort of recovery. In the night, I appreciate hymns such as "Abide with Me" to sing as prayers: "Abide with me, fast falls the eventide; the darkness deepens—Lord, with me abide; When other helpers fail and comforts flee, Help of the helpless, O abide with me."

If your mind is laden with anxieties tonight, pull out a hymnbook and try singing a favorite, or hum a song of praise, or make up your own song. Sing out loud or just sing within your heart. Like the psalmist, you can declare, "I sing in the shadow of your wings. My soul clings to you; your right hand upholds me."

Prayer

Thank you, Lord, for the gift of music. Draw me close as I sing to you tonight. Amen.

Listening

Read 1 Samuel 3:1-10.

> "Then Samuel said, 'Speak, for your servant is listening' "
> (v. 10).

The wail of a hungry infant, the cry of a child experiencing a nightmare, the shrill ring of a telephone—these sounds jolt us awake in the middle of the night. After we deal with the interruption (whatever it may be), we return to bed, but often we have trouble falling asleep again. Yet not too many of us have been awakened like little Samuel.

One night when the prophet Samuel was a child serving at the temple, a voice awakened him, not once but three times. It took time for Samuel to distinguish it from the voice of the old priest Eli and to recognize the voice of God. After all, he had never heard God's voice before, and one's perception is not always clear when one is tired. But when God called his name the third time, Samuel was ready to listen.

Might your wakefulness be a signal that God wants to get your attention? In the silence of the night perhaps a verse from the Bible will come to mind. Or you may think of particular friends out of the blue for whom you can pray. Maybe you will receive direction for the future or comfort through a present struggle. What could God be saying to you in the darkness of *this* night?

Prayer

Lord, I don't always hear you when you first call my name. Give me ears to listen to your still, small voice tonight. Amen.

A Midnight Snack

Read Psalm 1:1-6.

> "But his delight and desire are in the law of the Lord, and on His law—the precepts, the instructions, the teachings of God—he habitually meditates (ponders and studies) by day and by night" (v. 2, *The Amplified Bible*).

I'm not much of a midnight muncher, but many people are. Leisurely nibbling a midnight snack often soothes the sleepless. A bit of high-carbohydrate food can aid relaxation, making sleep come more easily. And perhaps the eating process itself makes us feel less alone. Perhaps with food we try to fill the emptiness created by a loss of sleep.

Another kind of food can help fill a hollowness within us too. The author of Psalm 1 speaks of meditating on Scripture, in a sense "feeding" on God's Word day and night. The writer describes specific benefits for those who make this part of their lives. What better time to practice meditation than during those otherwise unused hours when we can't sleep? Such quiet time provides an ideal opportunity to concentrate on a short passage of Scripture.

Another psalm says, "My eyes stay open through the watches of the night, that I may meditate on your promises" (Psalm 119:148). As one form of meditation, begin by reading a passage or verse several times, perhaps aloud. Ponder it, thought by thought, word by word. Commit the words to memory if you can. Next dig deeper, digesting the meaning of each word. What does it mean in the context here? What does it mean for my life now? Then wait for God to reveal an insight you might have overlooked without such attentiveness.

Tonight, along with your milk and muffin, try "chewing" on a bit of Scripture. By filling your spirit with a midnight meal of meditation, you will bear sweeter fruit for the kingdom of God.

Prayer

Lord, I offer tonight's wakeful hours to you by opening my Bible and meditating on your words. Fill me with your true "comfort food." Amen.

Nightlights

Read Psalm 8:1-9.

> "When I consider your heavens . . . the moon and the stars, which you have set in place" (v. 3).

In her book *Insomnia: God's Night School*, Connie Soth encourages insomniacs to go outside or sit by an open window and become acquainted with the "night personality" of wherever you live. Centuries ago, David did just that, as he looked at his night sky. Psalm 8 was his nighttime song of praise for God's glory as he saw it expressed in creation.

One predawn morning I decided to become acquainted with my neighborhood "nightlights," and I slipped out my back door. The moon, though a mere sliver, cast surprising brilliance across the landscape. The same stars I have often seen as tiny pinpricks of light in a canopy of sky shone in varying degrees of brightness against a deeper, vaster universe. Gazing up at the moon and stars, I was moved by the awesome beauty of creation and the God who brought it into being.

On the next clear night, when you find yourself awake, why not grab a jacket and go outside? Allow yourself to be awestruck by the majesty of God. Ponder his creation as displayed in the silent night sky and his touch in the heavenly lights above.

Prayer

O Lord, how majestic is your name. Thank you for calling me out of bed to witness your glory in the beauty of creation. Amen.

Decisions, Decisions

Read Luke 6:12-16.

> "Jesus went out to a mountainside to pray, and spent the night praying to God" (v. 12).

My husband and I had a big decision before us. We had prayed about it. We had compared lists of pros and cons. We had discussed the situation with our daughters and a few close friends. I had lost sleep over it. But as the hour of decision approached, we didn't feel assured of God's will in the matter.

We looked to the Bible for some wisdom. We read that when Jesus had a big decision to make—for instance, choosing twelve apostles from a large number of followers—he went out on a mountainside and spent the entire night in prayer. If the Son of God needed to pray through the night before acting, how much more did we need to do the same!

I don't know if Jesus received a vision, had an impression, or heard God's audible voice telling him what to do, but the next morning he acted with confidence. The men he appointed as his disciples proved with their lives that he had made wise choices.

Perhaps you are struggling with not knowing what to do or where to turn. Why not take some time to pray? Your nightly prayers may not produce a vision, and maybe you won't hear God's voice speaking to you out loud. But through intensive prayer you, too, can gain direction and confidence to act.

Prayer

Lord Jesus, as decisions weigh heavily on my mind and heart tonight, I choose to follow your example. I will spend more time praying for guidance than trying to sleep. Amen.

Pray on Purpose

Read Luke 22:39-46.

> " 'Why are you sleeping?' he asked them. 'Get up and pray so that you will not fall into temptation' " (v. 46).

How many nights have you lain awake bored, wondering how to pass the time? When my friend Lori can't sleep, she has learned to recognize that God may want her to pray for someone. "A person's name will come to mind," she told me, "and I don't have peace until I have spent time praying for them. Often I find out later that they especially needed prayer that night for some reason." This is a common experience for many people who have dealt with sleeplessness from time to time.

The Bible supports these experiences, declaring that there is a time to sleep and a time to pray. For example, on the night Jesus was arrested, he and his disciples went to the Mount of Olives. Jesus prayed, while his disciples fell asleep. Jesus urgently reminded them of the importance of praying at that moment, rather than sleeping.

106

On nights when you struggle to sleep, consider that perhaps you are awake for a reason. Think about a friend who might need prayer. Is someone you know ill, grieving a loss, or having a tough time? Remember your family, or pray for neighbors, friends, or coworkers. You may not be asleep, but God will bless the time you spend with him in this way.

Prayer

Keep me faithful in the night, Lord, so I won't be sleeping when you call me to pray. Amen.

Night Vision

Read Luke 9:28-36.

> "Peter and his companions were very sleepy, but when they became fully awake, they saw his glory" (v. 32).

If only Peter had had a camera that night—when he saw his teacher Jesus meet with Moses and Elijah, when Jesus' appearance took on a dazzling brightness. The dramatic scene could have been part of a Hollywood movie. There was light and there was action, but there was no hidden camera on the mountain that night. If Peter, James, and John had slept that night, we would have no record at all of this amazing event, when Christ's true glory was revealed.

But Peter and his friends almost missed the whole thing. It was the end of a long day, and they had just hiked up the mountain. They were exhausted and kept dozing off. When the intense light finally woke them fully, they saw Jesus conversing with the two famous historical figures, and the cloud of God's glory overshadowing them. God spoke:

"This is my Son, whom I have chosen; listen to him." And they did.

Nighttime, when it is dark and quiet, is a good time for God to show himself to us. Even if you can't sleep, you can open your eyes to God's presence. He may have a word of encouragement to help you through a dark hour or a bright revelation of himself to share with others. Don't be so distracted by your insomnia that you miss it.

Prayer

Father, tonight in the darkness, improve my night vision so I may see the light of your glory more clearly. Amen.

Trusting through Trials

Read Acts 16:22-34.

> "About midnight Paul and Silas were praying and singing hymns to God, and the other prisoners were listening to them" (v. 25).

What a night! Paul and Silas had been stripped of their clothing, beaten, and thrown into jail. They had hurt the "business" of some local slave owners by freeing their slave girl from a demonic spirit. So they were arrested and locked in an inner cell, their feet fastened securely in torturous stocks.

We might expect to see these wounded saints discouraged, nursing their wounds and quietly consoling one another. Instead, we find them having midnight prayers and singing hymns. Suddenly a violent earthquake shakes off their chains, freeing them. Rather than seizing the opportunity to escape their torture chamber, Paul and Silas corral the other prisoners and prevent their jailer from committing suicide. Their long night of sleeplessness pays off. By the next morning they have led the jailer and his family to faith in Jesus Christ.

When we're wounded by the world, what is our response—weeping or witnessing to our hope in Christ? self-pity or song? When we feel like the world is against us, when we are overwhelmed and exhausted, Paul and Silas show us the benefits of choosing what God wants to accomplish *in* us—joy—and *through* us—bringing others to himself. Perhaps you can use your nighttime wakefulness to help others in some way. Ask God about it, then pay attention to ideas and opportunities that come to you.

Prayer

Lord Jesus, enter my night of weariness and discouragement. As I choose to focus on you, to pray and sing praise, release my chains, heal my wounds, and help me lead others to the joy of your salvation. Amen.

A Song of Joy

Read Psalm 149:1-5.

> "For the Lord takes delight in his people; he crowns the humble with salvation. Let the saints rejoice in this honor and sing for joy on their beds" (vv. 4-5).

"Music is a fair and glorious gift of God," wrote Martin Luther in the sixteenth century. "Besides theology, music is the only art capable of affording peace and joy of the heart." Oh, the power of music! Our Creator instilled in us the ability to respond to musical notes. Strong compositions rouse us to action, while soft, rhythmic melodies soothe and uplift us.

We read in the Old Testament that when King Saul was tormented by an evil spirit, David played his harp. "Then relief would come to Saul; he would feel better, and the evil spirit would leave him" (1 Samuel 16:23). As a child, I often lay in bed listening to my mother play the piano in the next room. Even when I was upset, the music soon soothed me to sleep. And consider the dentists who offer patients headphones so they can listen to music during jarring procedures. Music serves as a distraction and keeps nerve receptors busy carrying enough messages to the brain to help block some of the fear and discomfort.

Set aside whatever is keeping you awake tonight and let music bring you comfort. You may recall old hymns that are dear to you or sing new songs of praise that help you worship God and lift your spirits. If you are alone, you may want to play the radio or listen to a tape. Instrumental or vocal, classical or contemporary, the one to choose is the one that works best for you.

Psalm 149 calls on God's people to remember the greatness of his salvation and, in response, "sing for joy on their beds." As you lie awake, join this chorus of praise and thanksgiving. You might just sing yourself to sleep.

Prayer

Lord, may I experience joy as I praise you with music, whether in a worship service led by choirs or singing alone in bed at night. Amen.

Wake-Up Call

Read Isaiah 50:4-5.

> "He wakens me morning by morning, wakens my ear to listen like one being taught" (v. 4).

After a restless night, my body feels dull, achy, listless. Instead of trying to project a positive mental attitude, I try to shut out the world. My facial expression and body language broadcast a silent but clear message: Please leave me alone!

Such an attitude threatens to discolor my entire day—and my family's as well. Those are the times I need to come to the Lord for a change of heart. By spending a few minutes reading the Bible and praying, even when I don't feel like it, I open myself up to a different outlook, a wider perspective, and greater possibilities for the day ahead. On my own I don't have the wisdom or strength—or sometimes even the desire—to change. But God works in mysterious ways to transform and renew me.

I find that when I read his Word, God meets me there. When I take time to listen, he speaks to me in surprising ways, guiding and refreshing my weary mind and body. Somehow when my spirit is renewed and my mind alert, my body cooperates.

Are you tired this morning? Did a wakeful night leave you ill-prepared to face today's challenges? Try opening your Bible, and be willing to receive the "word that sustains the weary."

Prayer

Lord, as I open your Word this morning, let me hear your wake-up call clearly. Let this small act of obedience allow me to receive what you give me for today. I want to live joyfully, even when I'm weary with little sleep. Amen.

Songs in the Morning

Read Psalm 59:16-17.

> "But I will sing of your strength, in the morning I will sing of your love" (v. 16).

Climbing out of bed the morning after a night spent tossing and turning can be torture. Gone is any possibility of another hour—or even five minutes—of needed sleep. Weak with weariness, we wonder, "Will I have enough physical and emotional strength to face this day?"

Once again David, the psalmist, has set an example for us to follow. He had a few bad nights, too. After a particularly difficult night when he was besieged with enemy attacks, David made a conscious choice to depend on God's strength, not his own. He had been brought safely through the night, and he recognized God's care for him. As David looked to the new day, he greeted the morning by singing praises for God's deliverance.

I confess that I find it difficult to follow David's example. To open my mouth in song rather than grumbling takes more willpower than I can usually muster after a sleepless night. But when I can force myself to sing of God's love and strength, I'm usually surprised at the outcome. Singing is energizing and spiritually uplifting. Singing has the power to lift our heavy hearts and focus our attention where it belongs. Give it a try!

Prayer

Lord, my Strength, I sing praise to you. I put this day into your strong and capable hands. As you guide me, I will follow, depending on you for strength. Amen.

Up with the Birds

Read Psalm 139:11-18.

"When I awake, I am still with you" (v. 18).

I love waking up on summer mornings. I welcome hearing the birds sing as they greet the day and go about their activities. But if I haven't slept well, their songs irritate me. I hear noise rather than music. Their cheery chirping grates on raw nerves and exposes my fears of facing the day ahead on insufficient sleep. Perhaps you've experienced these grumbly feelings.

Psalm 139 offers a remedy for facing the day. It tells us that King David often considered God's thoughts and deeds long into the night. With his mind focused on the Lord, he could awake alert to God's presence, knowing that God was with him.

When you wake up with the birds, do you hear God's voice or the day's noise? As with David, preparing to hear God's still, small voice might begin the night before. Bedtime and middle-of-the-night prayers

118

lead more naturally to morning prayers. When you think about God in the wakeful hours, you may be more open to receiving the blessings he has waiting for you in the morning.

Prayer

Lord of the morning, you have been with me through the night, and you will be with me in the day ahead. Help me turn to you rather than grumbling and fussing. Amen.

The Morning News

Read Psalm 143:1-8.

> "Let the morning bring me word of your unfailing love, for I have put my trust in you. Show me the way I should go, for to you I lift up my soul" (v. 8).

Some people just can't imagine starting a day without a cup of coffee and the morning newspaper. But does the news we receive in our morning paper give us what we need to get our day off to a *positive* start? Not always. News of wars, homicides, economic distress, and corruption does little to lift our hearts and minds, especially if we are tired to begin with. Let's consider how we can jump-start our day with more optimistic "news."

In Psalm 143 we hear the psalmist praying fervently through the night, looking for God's answer to come in the morning. Pursued by enemies and overwhelmed in spirit, he pleaded for God to preserve his life. The "morning news" David longed to hear was twofold. First, he wanted to hear that his enemies had been overthrown. Second, he sought guidance for the new day: "Show me the way I should go. . . . Teach me to do your will, . . . lead me on level ground" (vv. 8, 10). His night-time prayer was "Help!" His morning prayer was "Lead!"

If we have called on God for relief in the night, our morning prayers can reflect David's words of hope as well. God has sustained us through our frustrations and fears. And his morning news flash is that his love will never fail.

What does God have in mind for you today? Whatever it is, you can welcome it, knowing that the Lord will be with you.

Prayer

Lord, my morning prayer today is: Show me the way I should go. Teach me to do your will. Lead me on solid ground. Amen.

Transfusion for the Weary

Read Isaiah 40:28-31; 41:10.

> "Those who hope in the Lord will renew their strength. . . . They will run and not grow weary, they will walk and not be faint" (40:31).

You groan as the alarm clock goes off. You just got to sleep an hour ago! Your mouth feels dry as cotton. Your eyes burn. Your body is stiff and sore. You're not ready to dig into the responsibilities of a new day. Like someone who has lost a significant amount of blood and requires a blood transfusion, you need a "strength transfusion." But where will this come from?

The Bible gives us a place to begin: hoping in the Lord. God meets us in our weariness and can infuse us with spiritual and physical strength to face and accomplish whatever he sets before us.

François Fénelon wrote, "There is only one way to love God: to take not a single step without him, and to follow with a brave heart wherever

122

he leads." It takes courage to follow God wholeheartedly and to commit ourselves to loving and obeying him. So what keeps us from doing it? Are we afraid to leave our comfort zones? Do we think he will ask of us more than we are able to give? Will he make us go where we don't want to go?

Let Fénelon's words encourage you: "The love of God, which will make us conscious of God's love for us, will give us wings to fly on his way and to raise us above all our troubles." Rest in the Lord's love and find new strength for today.

Prayer

God, today I step out in faith that you love me and will be with me. As I gather together my meager scraps of hope, renew my spirit and lift me above my fears. Amen.

Breakfast

Read John 21:1-14.

"Jesus said to them, 'Come and have breakfast' " (v. 12).

My mother has always insisted that breakfast is the most important meal of the day. Most nutrition experts, physicians, and teachers agree. But many people aren't hungry when they first get up in the morning, especially after experiencing a restless night with little sleep. By midmorning their activity levels plummet and their stomachs rumble. So they grab a donut and a cup of coffee to ward off hunger pangs until lunchtime—not the healthiest way to begin an already energy-deficient day.

Jesus' disciples may have begun their days in similar fashion, grabbing whatever was available to eat. But one morning they had a breakfast they would never forget. They had just completed a night of unsuccessful fishing. Exhausted and discouraged, they began to row slowly toward shore. Before they reached land, Jesus called out and instructed them to cast their nets on the *other* side of the boat. They

tried it, and to their amazement, the nets filled so fast they couldn't haul it all on board. As they towed their valuable cargo to shore, Jesus had a breakfast of bread and fish grilled over a fire of burning coals awaiting them. How appetizing it must have smelled!

The risen Lord Jesus filled his disciples' nets and stomachs, but he didn't stop there. He went on to refresh their spirits with his presence. As you consider how to best get through your day, begin by eating a healthful breakfast. The day will look brighter to a nourished body and mind. And trust that Jesus will be present with you as you "break the fast" and begin the day.

Prayer

Lord Jesus, help me to honor my body's needs on this day. Provide for my spiritual refreshment as well. Amen.

Making the Days Count

Read Psalm 90:12-17.

> "Satisfy us in the morning with your unfailing love. . . .
> Establish the work of our hands for us" (vv. 14, 17).

Life is short. All too short. Does that observation make you want to leap out of bed to make the most of today? Probably not, especially if you haven't gathered enough sleep hours through the night. Lost sleep tends to make us lose perspective about the time allotted to us. But whether we spend our days changing diapers, managing a corporation, teaching, prescribing medication, or selling insurance, we all seek purpose in our work. According to the Bible, work has both dignity and purpose.

Psalm 90 talks about the brevity of life and about finding our purpose as we live out our fleeting span on earth. In verse 12, the psalmist asks God to "teach us to number our days aright, that we might gain a heart of wisdom." In our busy world we need God to help us maintain this eternal perspective, especially when we're tired.

In his book *A Long Obedience in the Same Direction*, Eugene Peterson observes, "Work is a major component in most lives. It is unavoidable. It can be either good or bad, an area where sin is magnified or where our faith matures. . . . We are reshaped through the days of our obedience."

Mornings give us a fresh start, a new beginning. They give us a sign that everything isn't over yet. God still has a purpose for us. We don't want to just keep busy but to be faithful. This process involves not just what we choose to do with our time, but *how* we do it. Quickly review your schedule at the beginning of the day. Pray for the people with whom you will interact; pray about the tasks you must accomplish and the projects—large or small—for which you are responsible. Ask the Lord to bless and establish everything you do today.

Prayer

Father, may I begin this morning remembering that, with your blessing, my smallest deeds will be established forever. Amen.

Pressing On

Read 2 Corinthians 6:3-10.

> "As servants of God we commend ourselves in every way,
> . . . in hard work, sleepless nights, and hunger" (vv. 4-5).

When a family member requires nursing care through the night, when a project at work or school demands hours beyond the usual, when a child is sick or a friend needs a listening ear—these are times we must keep going in spite of fatigue. But we needn't panic over our loss of sleep. While experts recommend that we establish a consistent pattern for sleep, they have found our bodies amazingly resilient to occasional interruptions in our schedules. We can and will accommodate irregularities as needs arise if some of that "sleep debt" is paid back within a couple of days.

Paul, the apostle, had to keep going in his line of work. He started churches and worked with people constantly. He listed sleepless nights as one of the ways he suffered in serving Christ, placing sleeplessness in the same category as being beaten, imprisoned, and hungry. If you struggle with insomnia, you know what he means.

It requires tremendous endurance to work effectively when we are run down by chronic tiredness. Paul was able to keep his goal in mind and push through it all with rejoicing. This is the attitude I want to adopt when nighttime wakefulness weakens my mind and body.

Are you in a situation that requires more than you have to give? Lean hard on Christ and keep going. When God calls us to serve, he will provide the grace and strength we need for each new day.

Prayer

Father God, thank you that you are with me. Help me to faithfully push through the tough times and do the tasks you have given me to do. Amen.

Opportunities

Read 2 Corinthians 12:7-10.

> "That is why, for Christ's sake, I delight in weaknesses. . . . For when I am weak, then I am strong" (v. 10).

I keep a notebook handy to write in during my prayer time each morning. It includes a thanksgiving list, which covers specific answers to prayer, the special people in my life, spiritual blessings, and such tangible things as good weather and good health. Not long ago I wrote out a different kind of prayer: "Thank you for my weaknesses. They remind me to depend on you instead of myself."

The apostle Paul has taught me to thank God for difficulties and weaknesses, to see them as opportunities for God to work in my life. Paul himself was certainly no stranger to suffering. He was persecuted, insulted, abandoned, shipwrecked, and beaten. Perhaps most frustrating to him, however, was a "thorn in his flesh, a messenger of Satan" that tormented him. Scholars cannot agree on what this "thorn" was, but whatever it was, Paul pleaded with the Lord to remove it.

But God replied no. Instead, he told Paul, "My grace is sufficient for you, for my power is made perfect in weakness." Paul accepted God's answer and then learned the secret of delighting in his weaknesses and difficulties. These hard things were really opportunities for God's power to be unleashed through him.

Do you feel that your insomnia is *your* thorn in the flesh that diminishes your attempts to live productively? Try writing out your frustrations. Even if you don't feel like it, begin to thank God for your sleep deprivation and what you have learned through it. Decide to live in his grace and power rather than your own. Even this "weakness" can be an opportunity for God to work through you.

Prayer

Lord, I accept each day you give me as an opportunity. Despite my insomnia, help me to rest in your power and follow where you lead. Amen.

New Every Morning

Read Lamentations 3:21-24.

> "Because of the Lord's great love we are not consumed, for his compassions never fail. They are new every morning; great is your faithfulness" (vv. 22-23).

Garfield, the comic-strip cat, is notorious for not wanting to get up in the morning. He is often pictured with a blanket pulled over his head, willing the day to go by without him. On mornings when I haven't slept well, I feel just like Garfield. I have a sleep debt to pay and few reserves to depend on. My emotions are fragile, my physical energy low, my motivation minimal. Yesterday's disappointments cloud my vision for what today may bring. "Why bother to get up?" I grumble, sinking deeper into my bed and my misery.

But wait! Before we lose hope, let's consider these amazing verses written in the prophet Jeremiah's book of "laments." Jeremiah is mourning the destruction of Jerusalem and the exile of his people. One way

132

Jeremiah was able to readjust his attitude toward his circumstances was by remembering that God's compassions are new every single morning and that they never fail.

We have the same God Jeremiah had, a God of hope and love and faithfulness, of fresh mercies and compassions for each new day. However, when we are tired and our life situations seem the most bleak, it's so difficult to remember this truth. If you have a big sleep deficit and feel fragile, read these verses again, memorize them, think them over. Reaffirm with the hymnist:

> Great is thy faithfulness,
> Great is thy faithfulness;
> Morning by morning new mercies I see;
> All I have needed Thy hand hath provided—
> Great is Thy faithfulness, Lord, unto me!

Prayer

Lord, your love never fails. Help me ponder what surprises you might have waiting for me today. Amen.

75 Ways to Get a Good Night's Sleep

1. Develop a relaxing bedtime routine to prepare your mind and body for sleep.
2. Establish a regular schedule for going to bed and getting up in the morning. A consistent wake-up time helps set your internal biological clock.
3. Don't sleep in on weekends. Keeping irregular hours undermines your ability to sleep soundly.
4. Reset your "body clock" with chronotherapy, which involves following a schedule of prescribed bedtimes that move backwards around the clock.
5. Don't panic if you lose a night's sleep once in a while. Occasional bouts of insomnia are normal.
6. Say your prayers. Praying for your family, your friends, and your world will take your mind off yourself as you bring others' needs before God.
7. Form bonds with other nonsleepers during the day. Pray for them at night when you can't sleep.
8. Take a bath before you go to bed to cleanse, warm, and relax your body.
9. Plan your next day's activities early in the evening, then mentally set them aside until the next day.
10. Allow yourself an hour to unwind before you lie down to sleep.

11. Drink a cup of warm milk or herbal tea.
12. Avoid fried, spicy, and other hard-to-digest foods that produce excess stomach acid.
13. If you need a snack, eat foods heavy in carbohydrates, such as a bowl of cereal, a light sandwich, a baked potato, some pretzels, or a couple of cookies. These are processed right away and help rush tryptophan, a sleep-inducing amino acid, to the brain.
14. Eat a tablespoon of honey before retiring. (A friend of mine swears by this.)
15. Don't drink lots of fluids after supper. You may awaken in the night needing to go to the bathroom.
16. Cut out caffeine for at least six hours before going to bed. It takes six to eight hours to eliminate the stimulant from your system. Even if caffeine doesn't interfere with your falling asleep, it might wake you in the night.
17. Say no to a nightcap. Alcohol may put you to sleep, but its rebound effect disrupts your deepest period of dream sleep.
18. Stop smoking. Studies show that because nicotine is a stimulant, smokers take longer to fall asleep and sleep more lightly than nonsmokers.
19. Rock in a rocking chair. John F. Kennedy used a rocking chair to soothe his back pain.
20. Practice relaxation techniques. For example, consciously relax your muscle groups one at a time or listen to relaxation tapes as you go to sleep.
21. Get some exercise every day so you will be physically tired at night.
22. Do some gentle stretches before you go to bed to relax tense muscles.
23. Do not exercise vigorously within three hours of bedtime.

24. Resist the urge to nap during the day. You might not be sleepy at night when you go to bed.
25. If you must nap, do so at the same time each day (but not in the evening), and then only for twenty minutes.
26. Allocate a specific time during the day to "worry." Don't save it for bedtime. Keep in mind that prayer is helpful in overcoming worry. Bring your worries to the Lord and leave them there.
27. Create a restful environment in your bedroom. Quiet colors and soft bedcoverings invite you to sleep.
28. Invest in a good mattress. It should provide enough support and space for maximum comfort.
29. Elevate the head of your bed to help digest food and prevent heartburn.
30. Rest your head on a comfortable pillow.
31. Invest in sleepwear that "breathes," like cotton. Make sure it's roomy, and cut off any tags that scratch.
32. Maintain a steady nighttime temperature in your bedroom—not too warm, not too cool. Sleep experts suggest the mid-60s.
33. Keep your feet warm. Soak your feet in warm water, or wear socks. (This can really make a difference!)
34. Darken your room with heavy draperies or blinds.
35. Listen to the quiet. Mask the noise of traffic, airplanes, and trains with a quiet fan or a machine that produces soothing sounds.
36. Wear earplugs if your spouse or roommate snores or grinds their teeth.
37. Play soft music, especially nocturnal music, such as Grieg's *Nocturne*,

Debussy's *Clair de Lune*, Palmgren's *May Night*, or one of your favorites.

38. Sing yourself to sleep. Soothing lullabies aren't just for children.
39. Practice breathing slowly and deeply, concentrating on each breath.
40. Hide your clock.
41. Find a companion—perhaps a teddy bear, a snoozing pet, a picture of a loved one, a radio or tape with earphones. Use your imagination!
42. If you feel insecure in your home or apartment at night, invest in a security system, smoke alarm, carbon-monoxide detector—whatever will ease your fears.
43. Don't watch TV in bed, and don't eat in bed.
44. Don't use your bedroom as a home office. You will be thinking about work instead of resting.
45. Read to relax before you go to bed (if you don't find it too stimulating!).
46. Reserve your bed for sleeping and marital relations.
47. Keep paper and a pen next to your bed and write down concerns, ideas, or other thoughts that trouble you in the night. Deal with them in the light of the next day.
48. Count sheep.
49. Count backwards slowly from 1,000.
50. Count your blessings. A thankful heart quiets the spirit.
51. Meditate on or memorize Scripture.
52. Think about friends from far away or long ago.
53. Imagine a lazy summer day. Feel the warm sun on your body. Picture yourself relaxing on a beach, listening to the waves.

54. Play mind games. For example, try to name all fifty states (or their capitals) in alphabetical order.
55. Process past experiences for good in your life. The middle of the night may be a suitable time for you to experience personal growth.
56. Recall a cherished memory.
57. Silently repeat a treasured Bible story or a favorite short story.
58. If you wake up and can't get back to sleep, get up and read (or organize your grocery coupons or clean out a drawer—something monotonous and nonstimulating) for twenty minutes or so, then go back to bed and try again.
59. Go outside and gaze at the splendor of the night—the stars and the moon. Listen to night sounds.
60. Wish on a star. Dreams are often born at night, to be realized in days ahead.
61. Use the undisturbed quiet of a sleepless night to develop your creative talents—write, paint, play an instrument (if it won't bother others), do needlework, etc.
62. Play with your hamster. Spending time with a nocturnal pet will help exchange your anxiety for a lighthearted and peaceful spirit.
63. Try taking an antihistamine. They tend to make you drowsy and are non-habit-forming. (Consult your doctor first.)
64. Ask your physician to check for medical causes of insomnia, such as sleep apnea, restless legs syndrome, fibromyalgia, etc.
65. If pain, fever, itching, or coughing interferes with sleep, treat the condition

rather than the insomnia. Pain relievers make excellent "sleeping pills."

66. Don't take sleeping pills without first consulting your doctor. Prescription drugs to induce sleep are more effective than over-the-counter remedies.
67. Check any other medications you may be taking to see if they contain stimulants or disturb sleep.
68. Consider psychiatric counseling to cope with depression, anxiety, or grief, which may be interfering with your ability to sleep.
69. Try a heating pad to relieve a backache. (Be cautious; follow instructions to prevent burns.)
70. Ask your physician about taking vitamin E or dopamine for restless legs syndrome.
71. Aim for *quality*, not necessarily quantity, of sleep.
72. Figure out by trial and error how much sleep you really need. It may be less than you think.
73. Keep a sleep journal for a couple of weeks to help identify trouble spots. Log how long it took to fall asleep each night, whether you ate before bed, how many times you awoke, how you felt in the morning, etc.
74. Visit a sleep center if your insomnia is frequent or prolonged.
75. Remember that you are not alone. One-half of the adult population in the United States struggles with sleep, and many are awake tonight.

When and Where to Seek Professional Help

If your sleep has been disturbed for more than a month and significantly interferes with the way you function during the day, you may want to consider getting professional help. Is falling asleep hard for you? Does it take you more than thirty minutes to fall asleep? When you wake up during the night, can you get back to sleep? Do your worries keep you awake? Do you feel tired in the morning even if you have slept? Do you wake up too early? If you can answer yes, these are some of the signals that indicate it may be time to seek medical advice.

Sleep disorders are diagnosed and treated by a variety of health-care providers, including general practitioners and specialists in neurology, pulmonary medicine, psychiatry, psychology, and many other fields. Begin by seeing your primary care physician. Your medical history, a physical exam, and laboratory tests may help to identify the problem, if it is a physical one. Tell your doctor if your insomnia makes you sleepy or depressed or otherwise affects your daily life. Before visiting your doctor, keep a diary of your sleep habits, showing your sleeping and waking patterns for a week or two.

Counseling or psychotherapy can help those people whose insomnia stems from underlying psychological or emotional factors. Depression is a leading

141

cause of sleep disorders and is often characterized by some of the following symptoms: persistent sadness, pessimism about the future, crying a lot, being easily irritated, low self-worth, and general malaise or disinterest in life. Counseling can also help someone coping with grief and loss.

To find a good counselor, consult the following: (1) your pastor, your doctor, or a friend whom you trust; (2) your health insurance company's list of providers; (3) state and national registers of therapists available at the public library (such as the National Register of Health Service Providers of Psychology). No matter whom you choose, you are entitled to get a second opinion and even change counselors if service is not satisfactory.

Some insomnia can be relieved by information and education. Getting "eight hours of beauty sleep" is a cultural maxim, but not always true. The amount of sleep different people require varies, and those who naturally sleep less merely need to abandon the myth that everyone needs eight hours of sleep. Do some reading and research on sleep. Experiment to find out what your body requires.

The American Sleep Disorders Association, founded in 1987, works to increase awareness of sleep disorders. The ASDA represents more than 2,250 specialists and researchers in sleep-disorders medicine.

For a list of accredited sleep-disorder centers near you, write to:

American Sleep Disorders Association
1610 14th Street NW, Suite 300
Rochester, MN 55901

For more information on insomnia, write to:
National Sleep Foundation
1367 Connecticut Avenue NW, Suite 200
Washington, DC 20036

For information available on the Internet, see:
National Sleep Foundation
URL: http://www.sleepfoundation.org

The Sleep Medicine Home Page
URL: http://www.cloud9.net/thorpy
This Internet site is sponsored by the Montefiore Hospital Sleep Disorder Center in New York and lists resources on all aspects of sleep. It includes a directory of discussion groups, mailing lists, sleep-related foundations, sleep-disorder centers and other sleep-related information.

Searle HealthNet
URL: http://www.searlehealthnet.com
The Searle Internet site includes a section on sleep-related information and news highlights from the nation's top media.

SleepNet
URL: http://www.sleepnet.com
SleepNet is a comprehensive site sponsored by the Stanford School of Sleep Medicine in California that links to information on support groups, sleep disorders, treatments, and sleep-disorder centers.

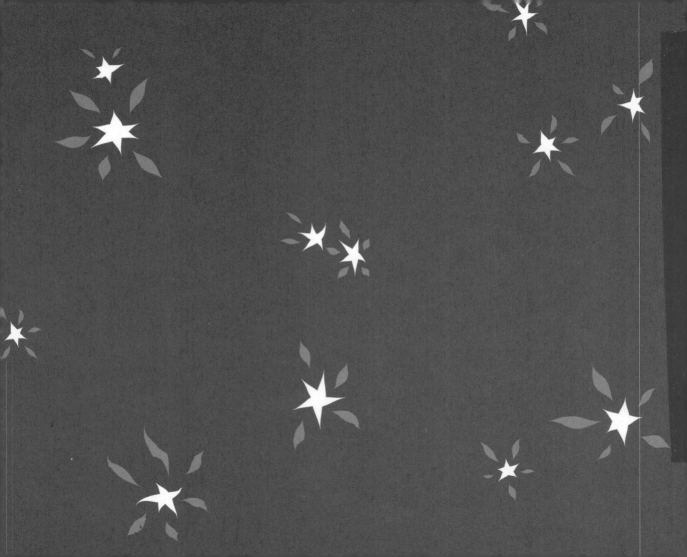